For Betty and Jim

God Bless You

Barbara Bosarge

Lament, Love and Laughter

BARBARA BUNTIN BOSARGE

LAMENT, LOVE AND LAUGHTER

Copyright © 2021 Barbara Buntin Bosarge.

All rights reserved. No part of this book may be used or reproduced by any means, graphic, electronic, or mechanical, including photocopying, recording, taping or by any information storage retrieval system without the written permission of the author except in the case of brief quotations embodied in critical articles and reviews.

iUniverse books may be ordered through booksellers or by contacting:

iUniverse
1663 Liberty Drive
Bloomington, IN 47403
www.iuniverse.com
844-349-9409

Because of the dynamic nature of the Internet, any web addresses or links contained in this book may have changed since publication and may no longer be valid. The views expressed in this work are solely those of the author and do not necessarily reflect the views of the publisher, and the publisher hereby disclaims any responsibility for them.

Scripture quotations marked NIV are taken from the Holy Bible, New International Version®. NIV®. Copyright © 1973, 1978, 1984 by International Bible Society. Used by permission of Zondervan. All rights reserved. [Biblica]

Any people depicted in stock imagery provided by Getty Images are models, and such images are being used for illustrative purposes only. Certain stock imagery © Getty Images.

ISBN: 978-1-6632-2521-4 (sc)
ISBN: 978-1-6632-2523-8 (hc)
ISBN: 978-1-6632-2522-1 (e)

Print information available on the last page.

iUniverse rev. date: 07/16/2021

My gratitude to those who encouraged and prodded, otherwise, this book would not be a reality.

The Land

When you look out on this land, you see trees, grass, buildings and fences. I look out and see so much more; memories are awakened, senses are heightened. There's heart and soul in this land. My great-grandfather walked this land. I never knew him, but I knew and loved my "Granddaddy and Grandma." I look out on pastures and fields and see a cotton field, "white unto harvest," and a small white country girl, dressed in a feed-sack dress, dragging a flour-sack cotton picking sack, surrounded by the blacks that lived on and worked this land. There was a relationship that few remember now. I don't remember thinking about race, they were people I knew and loved. I remember Uncle Henry, his wife, Lettie, their son and his wife, William Henry and Annie Mae. They also had a daughter named Mamie Lee, who lived away, but her daughter, Otha Belle, lived with Lettie and Uncle Henry most of the time and she was my best friend. Oh, how I loved them and that love was returned in so many ways. Lettie could bake the best sweet potatoes and corn bread. William Henry and Annie Mae had twin boys and they were just precious. I would bring a jar of beans or peas, Annie Mae would cook corn bread and I would spend the day with them and play with those babies.

Granddaddy

This land brings back memories of Granddaddy soaked with sweat in the sweltering Mississippi sun, plowing, planting, mowing and harvesting. Mid afternoon, I would draw a fresh bucket of water from the well, take Granddaddy a quart jar full, along with a plug of his chewing tobacco. I can see the grin on his face when he looked up and saw me coming. How I loved to ride to the cotton gin in the wagon, with Granddaddy. He would always buy my brother, Oliver, and me a treat: candy, either peppermint or a Tootsie Pop and sometimes even a Nu Grape or Orange Crush. Oh, how good it tasted. Granddaddy would play marbles with us, dig worms and take us fishing in Mr. Barber's pond. We'd climb on his old gray mare, Fannie, and all three of us would ride off. Memories of Granddaddy prompted me to write these words:

The Farmer

With dignity, he stood straight and tall
wearing faded work shirt, old patched overalls.
His calloused, wrinkled hands gripped the worn plow stock.
He scored the furrows deep and straight.
The sun beamed bright and hot,
sweat streamed from his brow.
His odor, while strange, did not offend.
Sunshine, sweat and freshly turned soil
was in itself a curious blend.

In spring he plowed and planted and dreamed a myriad of things
unspoken, perhaps yet revealed, a smile, half-hidden, a sigh,
a far away look in his eye.
The seeds that had lain dormant
were sprinkled by gentle rain,
stretched, burst forth with life again.

They cracked the crust of the rich brown earth,
reached up to the sun,
stood straight and green as rows of miniature infantrymen.
They grew to a size about knee-high.
The farmer again hooked up his plow,
with loyal mule and scooter stock,
a sprinkle of nitrate hand strewn,
swept clean the weeds, turned up the soil.
A job well done, he laid his crops by.

The summer sun and moisture there matured the corn and grain.
His sun-parched face seemed etched in stone,
strong, yet tender, warm, pleasant, not cold.
The years that were passing left him feeling old.

The autumn came with a hint of frost
and the harvest reaped that day
was the farmer, himself, as he lay
on the fertile brown earth
that for all of his life had served him so well.

Grandma

I can hear Grandma humming or singing some hymn, as she always did. I chuckle when I remember her hurrying; she didn't go any faster, she just hit her feet on the floor a little harder! Oh the lessons I learned, sitting on the front porch in the swing with Grandma. We'd watch for the postman most every day and when he brought the "Christian Observer", we'd read the children's word and picture story. Grandma said she had been an "old maid school teacher" when she married Granddaddy, a widower. She used her school teaching skills to teach me to read and write before I even started school. I recited the Child's Catechism when I was seven years old. She taught me to memorize verses and even certain chapters from the Bible. Amazingly, I still remember most of those. Grandma taught the same adult Sunday School Class at Prospect Presbyterian Church for over forty years. Everyone loved Miss Ruth.

Holy Chicken

For as long as I can remember, any preacher who found himself in proximity of Grandma knew he could come to Miss Ruth's for a meal and a bed. Grandma nearly always kept a chicken or two in a coup just waiting for the arrival of some preacher. My brother and I would laugh and say that when a preacher drove up, the chickens panicked, and headed for shelter. It seemed that shortly after a preacher arrived, a fire was started in the old wood stove, and Grandma went out, wrung a chicken's neck, cleaned it, and iced it down. She would then fry the most delicious golden brown chicken, brown gravy and biscuits. That was generally all she would fix for supper, but was it good! One night my brother and I were spending the night with Grandma and Granddaddy and we were all awakened by a commotion in the chicken house. Granddaddy got up, pulled on his overalls, grabbed his shotgun and headed for the chicken house. Of course, he expected some kind of varmint. I looked wide eyed at my brother and said, "You don't suppose a preacher drove up, do you?" We both got so tickled, we almost got into trouble. Anyway,

Granddaddy shot a huge chicken snake. We laughed about this for years.

Grandma gave me so much. Even today, I miss her and hardly a day goes by that I don't think of her and remember something about her.

Memories of a Child

The old house is empty now, the porch swing, long still.
In the twilight, I feel the warmth, love, mine long ago; another time.

Shadows lengthen. Breezes whisper secrets
only a child can hear.
The setting sun is soon swallowed by night.
Stars appear in the heavens. The man-in-the-moon seems to smile.

Night's chorus accompanied by nature's philharmonic begins its performance.
I hear a whippoorwill, lonely, sad the sound.
Back and forth, I feel the swing; chain squeaking, floor creaking; familiar----comforting.

Soft hands caressing, kind, gentle voice
casts a spell, calms fears, dispels tears.
Sleepily, I snuggle in a blanket of love.

Eyes closed, I can feel the peace, security---
mine at Grandma's side.
Memories beckon; years fade away; happy, free---
I'm a child!

The last few weeks of her life, this entire neighborhood, ministered to Miss Ruth's family in ways too numerous to mention. The day Grandma slipped into a coma is a day I'll never forget. Chris, who had grown up on this land, was helping me with Grandma. We'd just finished bathing her and she looked up with the brightest eyes, her face aglow with joy, and said, "Do you see Him? He's coming to take me home." "Who, Grandma?" I asked. "Don't you see Him? Jesus is coming." Then she started to sing: "On Jordan's stormy banks I stand and cast a wistful eye to Canaan's bright and happy land, where my possessions lie." She sang every word of every verse of that old hymn, then, she started with, "My Jesus, I love Thee, I know Thou art mine. For Thee all the follies of sin, I resign.

My gracious Redeemer, my Savior art Thou. If ever I loved Thee, my Jesus, tis now." Then she sang every word of every verse of that old hymn. Then she'd go back to "Bound for the Promised Land" and then to "My Jesus, I Love Thee". Over and over she sang the words, until mid afternoon; she peacefully slipped into a coma. This was Thursday and on Monday morning, as Chris and I bathed her, she went home to Glory.

At the funeral home, everyone commented that when you looked on Miss Ruth's face, you couldn't grieve. She was radiant and had a peaceful smile on her lips.
Home sweet home!

Years after Grandma and Granddaddy died, my family had gone back to Prospect Presbyterian Church for "Homecoming and Dinner on the Grounds." Many reminisced about Grandma and Granddaddy. My heart was full and my eyes were swimming. On the way home, we would pass Grandma's and Granddaddy's old home, and as we went by, the following words flooded in and I had to hurry in to get a pen and paper so I could capture them.

Dear Old House

Dear old deserted house, it hurts me so
to gaze upon your emptiness and know
That once I loved your weathered walls,
played and danced throughout your halls.

To you I came with cares and pain,
Knowing I could find shelter from the rain.
You loved me when I felt no one could.
When things seemed unbearable, you made them good.

It was here I learned faith in God,
Learned to treasure and love the sod.
I loved your daffodils in spring, goldenrods in fall.
Thanked our Heavenly Father for making them all;
cows out in the barn, horses in the pasture,
Sunsets at evening we beheld in so much rapture.

Many things are in my memories today,
Though I guess this what I want to say.
You wonder how a house could make me love it so.

It wasn't the house, I'm sure you know.

It was those who lived, loved, and laughed there.

They taught me the right things to do,

A dear and precious Grandmother and Granddaddy, too.

Daddy

Where do I start? Daddy is 90 years old now and a resident of Kings Daughters and Sons Nursing Home. He has a form of dementia similar to Alzheimer's. The day I took him away from home for the last time, I penned these words:

Regrets

Why do I now feel so sad?
I grieve for the Dad I never had.

Memories of abuse, anger, rage
flood my thoughts and fill the page.

Life's a stage, we play our part,
the script's engraved on a broken heart.

With great effort, forgiveness came
as I struggled through a slough of pain.

Regrets will ever haunt my soul.
Abuse will always take its toll.

I see him old and for true it's sad
to grieve for the Dad I never had.

Some years ago, when I began to work on forgiveness and recovery, I wrote these lines. They were used in Newsletter of the Mental Health Association in Lauderdale County, Mississippi, as the focus for 1990 was the "Year of the Child".

Silent Cry

Eyes downcast, swimming in pools of sorrow.
What unspeakable horror haunts you?

Little shreds of secrets you scurry to cover.
Storm clouds billow. Rage pounds like hail.
Pain rips as wind whips branches in a storm.

Lying all around; fear, guilt, shame.
Deep within you cry; make it stop!

No one does. And it happens again -
And again.

You become a statistic; another victim.
Teacher, did you realize?
Neighbor, did you hear the cries?
You, who suspected, knew;
how do you feel?

Limp little rag-doll broken and still,
It's over.

Appalled, we wring our hands and weep.
But unless someone
does something,
it will happen again -
and again –

These words were written about Brent, my young cub scout wearing his uniform for the first time.

Cub Scout

Little boy growing old
Wearing Cub Scout blue and gold

Yesterday, Daddy's joy
Healthy, bouncing baby boy.

Today, mature and worldly wise
Full grown man, just half-pint size.

Heavy Heart

The heaviness
weighs upon me;
my head,
my limbs,
heavier still
my heart.

Lord of the
easy yoke,
Jesus, with promise
of burden light,

I cry to you
this endless night.

This son of mine,
of Thine….
My heart so filled
with love….
I know I must
let go.
Not abandon,
but release
to Your
merciful hand.

Keep him close,
protect and heal.
In his despair
help him feel
the pain.
Lean in to,
not flee
and hide,
but crying out

be drawn
to You
and there
abide.

Written March 11, 1994. Six days later on March 17, 1994, on his 28th birthday, my son, Brent, took his life.

One morning about two years after my son's suicide, I was walking early, as usual. This is my time with God and it seemed in those years since Brent died, all I could do was cry. The thought came to me that I had used up a lifetime of tears and couldn't one just exhaust the supply? No, I knew better. But on this particular morning, I began to observe a butterfly. I never realized before that butterflies glide on wind currents and really don't do a lot of flying. Once conscious of the butterfly, I began to think that maybe God was speaking to me through this creature. The message: No matter how dark the gloom or deep the grief, there is still beauty. A butterfly is a thing of beauty. Even peering through tears, the scene is enhanced by light refracting through the droplets, much like a rainbow. I became entranced. My focus had shifted and now I could see beauty! Thank you, God.

Another message was that though we struggle, "quiver, thrash", and even almost "crash", God is still there and His love and power will see us through. In retrospect, the last door in the stages of grief, acceptance, opened ----just a crack perhaps, but never the less I desperately needed the light that peeked through.

As I returned home that morning, these are the words that came:

On Wings

The early morning rays of sun
filter through the mist.
On unseen wind you float;
then
        downward
                drift,
till wings of amber and ebony
stroke the air, catch the wind, glide free.

I watch and think of me.

Trusting Him I glide
on wings of faith.
Earth's downward pull prevails.
On my own strength I quiver, thrash,
then about to crash - -
I catch the wind.
His love, His power, transcend.

Metamorphosis

Brown
and
lifeless-
seeming
pod
clinging
to
the
twig.

Silken
case
of
pupal
shell
is
cracked
by
life
within.

Jeweled
wings
expand,
contract,
emerge
to
freedom's
light
and
fly
away.

For the past ten days, I've kept my grandson, Haze, while my son, Brian and his wife, Laura, were on an elk hunt in Colorado. Haze; who will be five the end of the month, is a joy to his Paw and me, but is such an energetic little fellow that he keeps us in high gear. I've found that if he is kept busy and challenged, he does extremely well. For some time, I had planned activities that do just that. Knowing those ten days to two weeks is a long time for a little boy to be separated from his Mom and Dad; several projects were planned as surprise welcome home gifts for them. Things had gone well and I had had few problems with discipline.

About the eighth day, it seemed he had broken, bent or otherwise damaged several things and I gave him a pretty stern lecture about handling things that he didn't know about. I told him if he didn't have permission, to ask before he even touched them. Within minutes, I discovered a piece of wood that had been broken into three pieces. For a second, I questioned what it was, and then I knew.......

Six and a half years ago, we lost our younger son, Brent, at 28 years of age. Shortly after his death, I brought in a bird feeder that was in need of repair and placed it in the patio closet. When Brent was about eight or ten years old, he had ordered a kit that contained a bird house and a bird feeder. He had done this without my knowledge, assembled them and gave them to me as a gift. Needless to say, after his death, they became treasures. The birdhouse had sat on the top shelf of a baker's rack on a covered patio, so it was excellently preserved. The feeder; however, had hung in a tree and the weather had taken its toll. Several weeks ago, I had retrieved the feeder from the closet, carefully taken it apart, removed the rusty nails and screws, and cleaned and sanded the pieces. I planned to use a good quality wood preserver and reassemble it. Having left these pieces on the baker's rack, Haze had picked up one and broken it into three pieces. Tenderly, I picked up the pieces and asked Haze why he had done this. He shrugged his shoulders and replied, "It was no good." I told him the story of Brent's having made it for me and how it was now a treasure. As I spoke, the tears started. I said no more, got the wood glue, a wet cloth, my box of C-clamps and went outside and sat in the drive way.

The tears would not stop as I anxiously struggled to put it back together. If you've ever worked with anything like this, you know that two pieces are relatively simple to glue, but because of the way the pieces had splintered, I knew if I glued two pieces back, the pressure from tightening them together would damage the splintered edge. This would make the repair obvious when I glued the third piece. So with trembling fingers and tear-filled eyes, I struggled. Haze stood near bye, motionless and silent. Suddenly, he ran around the corner of the house, out of sight. Almost impatiently, I thought, "Now, I'd better stop and check on him." Just then, he ran back. Smiling confidently, he put his arm around my neck, patted my shoulder and said, "Grandma, I said a prayer for God to help you put it back together." Miraculously, the three pieces slipped into place, the C-clamps tightened, and everything remained perfectly aligned. I lay down the piece of wood, took that precious little boy in my arms and the tears really came then. "Thank you for your prayer and thank you for reminding me that God is always near, ready to help us do what we alone can not do," I whispered.

Now I have a true treasure in that bird feeder; built with love by one little boy, repaired with love and God's help through the faith-filled prayer of another little boy.

Lines on Wynn Bullock's Photograph, "Forest"

I enter uninvited
Quietly, reverently
Ethereal cathedral
Mist embraced
Spires reaching upward
Sun's fingertips gently touch

With brightness and beauty
The lush, verdant view
Fern-fronds beckon escape
From humanity's madness

The cool, quiet stillness
The solitude
The enduring strength and majesty
Of this resplendent place
Fill me with awe and wonder
I wait…
I feel Divinity's Presence

Oliver

It was rage that fueled his obsession with winning and being the best; the

rage of a helpless little boy at the hand of a violent and abusive father. In

the end, it was rage that stilled his heart.

Easter Orchid

Such a waste, she said wistfully as she viewed the lovely white orchid pinned to my shoulder. Waste? No------extravagance, maybe-------but waste? Never. As she walked sadly away, my thoughts turned to the woman who came with an alabaster jar of very expensive perfume. She broke the jar and poured the perfume on Jesus' head. Why had she done this? Her act was questioned and considered a waste also. But what had motivated this bold act? Was it not love, gratitude? This was Jesus, her Lord. Jesus said, she has done a beautiful thing to me. This is precisely the way I feel each Easter when that orchid arrives.

Year ago, on the first Easter that found my daughter so many miles from home with a husband and young son, the phone had rung just as we sat down to lunch. Mother, she sobbed, I just want to tell you I appreciate you! All those years when everyone had new outfits, Easter baskets, colored eggs, a spotless house, such a delicious lunch after church; I guess I thought the Easter bunny did it all! The truth is I never really thought. But today, I realized it was you! Did you ever get to bed the night before? I'm so tired, Mother. I tried to do the things you always did and I'm exhausted. How did you do it? How? There's only one answer, love of course. Each Easter as I pin on my orchid, I know this her way of saying, Thank you, Mother. I love you.

As I view this fragile white flower, I'm also reminded that many of the truly precious things of life as just as short-lived as this blossom; a sunrise or sunset, a smile on a little one's face, the way the earth looks fresh-washed the moment the sun appears after a shower, the love in a husband's eyes, the pride on your son's face after a job well done, kind, gentle words; so many things. But their brevity in no way diminishes their joy. Remember this and treasure your orchids.

AUNT BARBARA'S THOUGHTS OF AUDRA

June 15, 2004

For the last few days, I've heard many words used to describe Audra, but none of them really say it. They're all true, but they're not nearly enough. Some I've heard are: "unique, special, generous, loving, caring, a sweetheart". To know Audra was to love her. And she certainly knew how to love you back. With Audra, "what you saw was what you got!" There was nothing fake about her. She accepted and loved everyone exactly the way they were. She didn't care who you were, where you lived, what you wore, or what you drove! When Audra walked into a room, you felt the power of love; and it was unconditional!

I've also heard, "she had a heart as big as all outdoors, and she had a heart of gold". As I thought of her, I wondered how one human body could contain such a big heart ...but I knew, it filled her up and overflowed. All who knew her and loved her were recipients of that overflow. When Audra hugged you, let me tell you, you had been hugged! She was the best hugger! I'll miss that.

Audra loved home and family. Many times she has told me of great times with her family. One of the reasons she quit driving a big rig was because she often found herself too far from home and family and for too long.

Audra loved her country. She was fiercely patriotic. I'm told she had a temper and if you disrespected our flag, our military, or anybody she cared about, look out! Don't try to take advantage of her, family or friend either or you just might see that temper flare!

Audra or Cookie as so many called her, was also fun, funny and she could be downright goofy! There's not a single person who knew her who will not smile or even have a big laugh when they recall some Cookie comment or escapade. Even with tears in my eyes, my heart smiles when I remember her.

She was the most giving person I've ever known. She could do almost anything; from driving a nail to backing a twenty foot cattle trailer into a glove-like opening. She often did these things for others. No one was surprised that she died, just as she lived…helping someone else and as a donor, she goes on giving and helping.

Audra loved life; she preferred adventure over a life of ease. In her spirit there was a love of wonder, an amazement at the stars and all of nature, an unfailing child-like appetite for what-next, and joy in the game of living. Audra packed more living into her 37 years than some do in long lifetimes.

Audra loved life, she loved people, but she always knew heaven was her home and though we weep, the angels rejoiced as they welcomed her home.

The last conversation I had with Audra was just before she left for California. She called and asked, "Aunt Barbara, will you do me a favor?" "If I can", I replied. "Will you record all of President Reagan's funeral services for me?" "Sure, I'll be glad to." "Thanks, Aunt Barbara, I knew I could count on you. I love you." "I love you, too. Be safe." For the first few days after the accident I was absolutely haunted by those words, "Be safe". Then in the middle of the night as I lay there thinking about her and replaying those last words, I guess I had an epiphany. Audra is safe, safe for eternity, safe in the arms of Jesus.

I love you, sweet girl.

Today, while sewing, I became quite impatient with the thread that repeatedly became knotted. Then I remembered one of my Grandma's favorite stories about something I had said as a little girl.

Growing up, I spent many happy hours sitting in the swing on the front porch with Grandma. She would read to me, tell me stories, share her faith in God and teach me many things. Maybe the biggest attraction was that she had time for me and I knew she loved me unconditionally. Grandma often did needle work, crocheting and embroidering, and one day, her thread continually became tangled and knotted. She said that as she became more and more irritated with this inconvenience, I asked, "Grandma, why does your thread keep making all those pretty little flowers?" I can remember the sparkle in her eyes, how she chuckled, and then reached over and gave me a big hug. I heard her tell that story many times and today as I became exasperated with my thread in the same way, I realized why she treasured that story so. It has to do with attitude and perception.

Here I sat in my comfortable home, well lighted sewing room, before a modern sewing machine, with drawers full of fabrics, thread of almost every color, and my thread kept making "pretty little flowers". Many of our irritations would seem "pretty little flowers" to those who struggle just to survive, who are experiencing neglect, abuse, disabling illness, severe financial reversals and other struggles.

I paused and thanked God for all "the pretty little flowers" in my life and especially for a Grandma, who loved me and loved and shared her Lord.

Sunrise Comes Softly

Night blankets the earth.
A halo of pink crowns the eastern horizon.
Silently, color rises;
Gilded shades of pink, coral, rose.
Night gives way to light.
Sun's rays pierce the veil.
Day is born as sunrise comes softly.

July, 2004

The early morning mist rises above the mirrored surface of the water.

Waves ripple as reflections create diamonds sparkling in the sunlight.

Morning has dawned, replacing the stars and moon of night.

Creatures of the day begin to stir, awakened from their slumber.

Your Spirit, Oh God, touches as a gentle breeze and
I am again awed by the beauty of Your creation.

Dear Haze,

Do you remember Saturday when you spent the night with us and you wanted to stay up later and Paw was tired and wanted to go to bed? As we well know, you do not turn on a light that might shine and wake up Paw! When you had finished watching the movie and were ready to go to bed, you wanted to turn on the light. I put my hands on your shoulders and guided you into your bed in the darkness. You made it in safely and I tucked you in.

I've thought about that a lot this week. That experience is really an example of faith. You had faith that as long as Grandma's hands were on you, you were safe, even in the darkness. When I was talking to you about this, you said, "But Grandma, I bumped into the bed, just a little." That is so like life. If we stay close to God, feel His hands on our lives, we're safe, even in the darkness. That doesn't mean, we won't have a few bumps, but as long as we stay close to Him, He'll help us over the bumps. How foolish it would be to pull away and stumble around, yet, in many ways we do just that.

My prayer for you is that you will stay close to God and even at times when you're uncertain or frightened, just lean back into His loving, secure arms and He will take you where you need to go.

Shalom.

I love you very much.
Grandma

Holy Week Reflection

The week that started triumphant
is now a dark, fearful time.
Jesus of Nazareth, betrayed, condemned,
His broken body on a Roman tree,
the cross of Calvary.

Good Friday, result of fear, pain,
sin committed by us, borne by Him.
Radical love misunderstood.
Love that stands
between the darkness and the dawn,
between death and life.

Holy Saturday, Easter Vigil;
disillusionment, fears and grief,
season after anguish, the experience
before the dawning of new life.

We wait.

We wait for the Lord.

We wait for hope.

Sabbath has passed.

Now, early morn, at the tomb

we hear the angel say,

"He is not here.

Come see where he lay.

He is risen, as He said.

Go and tell that others may know

He lives."

Homily of Wisdom for Youth, presented by Barbara Bosarge, Baccalaureate Sunday, May 1, 2005 at First Christian Church, Meridian, MS.

I once read that in the deep wisdom of life there are things to be learned that cannot be taught. We never know them by hearing them spoken, but we grow into them by experience.

A few weeks ago when Charlie asked me to share with you some wisdom from my life, I immediately thought of the fact that Parson Tom often mentions that we each have a story. So this is a chapter in my story that has taught me as no other.

Bo and I are the parents of three children, Renee, Brian and Brent. Our youngest son, Brent, suffered from a terrible disease, addiction. He spent his 18th birthday in Alcohol and Drug Rehab, and the next 10 years were a living nightmare. Brent would enter 8 more treatment programs. Some he completed, some he didn't. I watched my son hurt, struggle, fail, hurt, struggle, and fail again and again. He told me often of his sorrow for causing such pain to those of us who loved him most. Then, on March 17, 1994, on his 28th birthday, Brent took his life. To say I was devastated is a gross understatement.

As we entered the funeral home, I told God I can't do this. I didn't feel I could even breathe. There were no audible sounds, no angels, no visions, but in a quiet voice, I heard, **"Just lean on Me and I'll be with you."** That's exactly what I did. I leaned on Him. Do you remember when you were a child and learned to swim and float on your back? When you learned to float, you were told to just lean back on the water and relax. I had great difficulty with that. I would lean back, relax, sink a little, then I'd feel that I just had to do something; I'd struggle, sink and start over. Faith is something like that. We have faith, we know we do, things happen, we feel that we have to do something, we struggle and start over. Each time we go through some difficulty, our faith is strengthened.

God got me through the next days and weeks as I leaned on Him. The weeks turned into months, then years. In retrospect, I think that I shut down, emotionally and spiritually. It hurt too badly to think and feel, so I tried not to.

Slowly joy seeped back into my life and I began to think and feel again. As I look back over the events of our time with Brent, two things stand out. It's true that Brent disappointed me, hurt me, embarrassed me and literally broke my heart; but nothing he did altered the fact that he was my child and I loved him. Then I reasoned that if I, an earthly parent could love like that, how much our Heavenly Father must love his children. We are His children.

In Romans we read that we have received the **"Spirit of sonship. And by Him we cry, Abba, Father. The Spirit himself testifies with our spirit that we are God's children."** Romans 8:15b-16 NIV

Later in that same chapter, we are told that **NOTHING can separate us from the love of God that is in Christ Jesus our Lord.** Romans 8:39b NIV

In 1st John we read, **"How great is the love the Father has lavished on us, that we should be called the children of God. And that is what we are!"** 1 John 3:1 NIV

Always remember how you are loved! As you begin a new chapter in your story, the road won't always be smooth and straight, you will encounter bumps, some detours, and even a few bridges out.

In the end everything will be all right. Nothing can harm you permanently. No suffering is irrevocable, no loss is lasting; no defeat is more than temporary, no disappointment is conclusive. There is absolutely nothing in life or death that will ever come between you and the love of God made visible in Christ Jesus.

This was written with the help and encouragement of Jessie Lewis, and presented at the first PTA meeting of the year, probably in the mid to late 1960s.

The summer has been long and hot
Our well laid plans have gone to pot

The children have had their troubles too
Same ole complaints, there's nothing to do

We've pulled our hair and wished for fall
The first day of school, best day of all

And so tonight, I'd like to say
You're as welcome, teachers, as the flowers in May

We salute you for all you've tried to do
For the children and for the parents too

For your patience, your courage, hats off we say
Our debt to you would be hard to repay

The task you have is just stupendous
The things we all expect from you are tremendous

We ask you to take our Johnny and Sue
And make them over just like new

To our amazement, often you do
And our words are very small pay

We want you to know that in just every way
We're glad you're with us

We thank you for all
The ways you straighten them out in the fall

So here's to our teachers
May your tribe increase

At home there is silence
But also sweet peace

A Mother's Heart

Sleep well, my son. I wonder if I'll ever overcome the habit of checking to be sure you're covered, or maybe just to be sure you're there, safe. Oh! How you've grown—I can remember so well how I was so irritated when adults would exclaim, "My! Haven't you grown" and here I am, saying the same thing. I would think, "If I hadn't grown, then you would have something to get excited about".

Where have the years gone? It seems only yesterday, the nurse presented me with this perfect, beautiful creation of God. My first born son, living testimony of the love your parents have for each other. I'm glad you sleep for you would not believe how your mother could babble so.

Beautiful baby, curious toddler, when did you take that giant step from babyhood to boyhood?

I remember so well a dear elderly friend so often commented on how pretty you were; then one day in a tough little voice I heard you exclaim, "Me not pretty, me handsome!" No, you were a pretty baby no longer, now you were a handsome boy.

The years passed so swiftly; my baby going to school! It can't be. I will never forget putting you on that bus for the first time. I felt as though a huge yellow monster had devoured my baby. I climbed the driveway, my eyes overflowing with tears. Not so tightly, mother, loosen the apron strings, I told myself.

Then in rapid procession football, basketball, baseball, what ever the season, your 4H camp, all the activities of a growing boy. Oh, what pride I felt when your 4H leader called just to tell me what a joy you were, and how your respect for adults had impressed her. There is still so much pride in my heart as I gaze into your innocent face. Look at that tousled hair. Ah, something seems different. Baby…….. Boy………. Man………? My son, a man? Oh no! Not yet, but……….somewhere between boy and man. Will I know son, the instant you cross that threshold? I think not. But even if I don't know the exact instant, one day, I'll realize you have crossed over. Time is such a sneak, always lurking behind, ready to pounce forward at the most unexpected time; my little boy, no more; my son, forever.

What a foolish old mother you have. Thank God you have a wise and loving Heavenly Father. Your daddy and I have loved you so, perhaps unwisely, but I hope you will always know there is One, Who loves you wisely and well. Son, as you become a man, may you always follow as He guides. I wish for you so many things; success, love and happiness. But if you make happiness a goal, it becomes elusive. It seems to be the byproduct of a good life. "Seek ye first the kingdom of heaven and all things will be added unto you."

Sleep well, my son, the hour is late and your mother's heart is filled with love, not always patient, kind and long suffering; but when you become a father, you will better understand.

    Written when my son, Brian, was about fifteen.

We bought a 35mm camera and during my children's growing up years, I took color slides. Every time we had a family gathering, everyone would say let's look at your slides and I would get out the Kodak carousel projector and some trays of slides, pull down the screen and begin the viewing! It was really fun and you could watch the children grow up and the adults grow old! On one occasion, the slide that appeared on the screen was of our youngest, Brent, who was just over a year old. Here was this precious toddler standing before a "Pride of Mobile" azalea in full bloom. It was a beautiful slide, the kind that you see on a calendar. Everyone was oohing and aahing and just totally admiring the photo and above everyone, I heard Brian, then about 9, say, "Good gosh, look at the nut grass!!!" Sure enough, poking up their little green shoots through the pine straw mulch was nut grass!!! I've thought of this often over the years and I realize that at times we all have a tendency to focus on the nut grass instead of the goodness and beauty with which we're so blessed. What are the reasons for this? I'm sure Brian just didn't want Brent getting all the attention.

But sometimes I have to face the fact that I'm inclined to have a critical spirit and I really wish I didn't.

When my first child, a daughter, was six or seven years old, the children in her class were asked what they wanted to be when they grew up. Almost without exception, the girls answered either a school teacher or a nurse. The only exception was my daughter, Renee, who wanted to be a Saloon Girl like Miss Kitty on Gunsmoke. When asked why, she replied, "She always wears pretty dresses, her hair is always pretty and she doesn't have to work"! This child has always been a free thinker and never hesitated to share her opinion.

A few years later, when our house was on the market and we needed to sell it to get the equity, so that we could start building on land we had acquitted, the REALTOR brought a nice couple over. The man remarked that everything looked newly painted, Renee said, "Oh, it had to be. There were holes in all the walls, but Mama hid them!" I explained that the previous owners had no doorstops and the doorknobs had punched holes in the sheetrock, I had patched and repaired them. The couple had lived in Central America for over twenty years and had no experience with heat, so they were inquiring about the home heating. Before I could answer, Renee said, "Oh, you will freeze, it's all broken!"

At this time, my son was a little over one year old, and a very active toddler. Being afraid he might turn the gas on, I had removed the handles for the floor furnace and the gas bathroom heater during the summer. I quickly took the handles out and showed them how to replace them. It seemed that everything they asked about, Renee had an answer! I kept trying to get her to go play, but to no avail. Then the question was asked. "What about the neighbors"? Before I could answer, Renee piped in, "Oh, they steal everything. They even stole my Daddy's pants". This caused me to explain that my husband used this comment when he couldn't find something. He would say, "I don't see them. Somebody must have stole them"! Finally they left and I just knew I would never hear from them again. Surprisingly, within an hour, the REALTOR called and had a contract! At the closing, the buyers chuckled about our daughter and said that she had sold the house! They were confident that if anything had been really wrong, she would have told them!

During her teen years there were challenges, but we both survived! Today, I am so proud of the woman she is! We can laugh at many of her comments and experiences. She has told me repeatedly, "You did teach me to be truthful!"

Dear Kalen,

The corona virus has altered many things in our lives but it cannot alter our memories.

I remember a little girl about two years old who after her bath, Grandma wrapped in a soft blanket and carried her out to the front patio to listen to friendly night sounds. The nighttime insects and frogs seemed far enough away to be safe, when an owl lit on a fence post right in front of where Kalen and Grandma were sitting. The owl's "Who Whos, Awho" was so very near and loud that Kalen's eyes widened, and she exclaimed, "Not me like friendly night sounds."

While staying in a cabin on the Mitolius, Grandpa decided to go for a walk. Pre-school Kalen wanted to go too. Grandpa told her she would have to walk, that he couldn't carry her. As they walked, Kalen tiring, she began to lag behind. In a pleading little voice, she said, "If you 'care-we' me, I will give you kisses." Grandpa "care-weed" her.

So many memories; so much love. Thank you precious granddaughter. Happy Birthday!

Love, Grandma and Grandpa

Dear Will,

I really think I should title this, the same as Bob Hope's theme song, *Thanks for the Memories*! Where have the years gone? I owe you thanks for creating the most rewarding role of my career, in this drama of life, "Grandma"! It is certainly my favorite.

When you were just a baby, your parents came for a visit. I think you were living in Terrell, Texas, and you were so fussy. As I held you, your little head against my shoulder, you would stop crying and go to sleep. But if I tried to put you down or hand you to your Mother, you would start crying again. I told her that you had an ear ache, and a doctor's visit confirmed this. The warmth of my body next to that aching ear gave relief. I thought for a moment, just being in Grandma's arms was all you needed! (Not really)

The time passed quickly and then you were just a couple of years old and Grandpa and I can still see you in our living room, with those big, soulful eyes, singing *Annie's Song*! Those eyes could have melted an iceberg. Al Gore knows nothing about *global warming*! Then as time passed, you would sing *King Tut* and *The Gambler*. Grandpa's and my favorite lines were, "then he <u>bombed</u> a cigarette and asked me for a light."

After you moved to Oregon, Renee sent a cassette tape of you all discussing your first trip to the beach. Your mom asked you what you wanted to say to Grandma and "Daddy-Daddy" and you said, "Dey say dey saw a whale, but I don't believe 'em!" We wore that tape out listening to that line.

Thank you for coming to visit in the summer, the hot Mississippi summer. You concluded early that harvesting corn, "was no fun!" I remember one night you decided to go to bed with "Daddy-Daddy" and after a short while, you came into the den, with eyes as wide as saucers and exclaimed, "Gramma, how do you sleep with that man?" He had had one of his nightmares and was kicking and yelling out and to be honest, I had sometimes wondered that question, myself! Then there was the time, when I had had my bath and I always slathered myself with lotion. You were sitting beside me on my bed, and rubbing my arm and you said, "Gramma, why do you always feel moldy?"

The time moved on and you went to Space Camp at Huntsville, Alabama. On one of our trips to Gulf Shores, Alabama, you and Kalen decided to go in just after I had gone to the beach. I had placed a fairly large cheese ball covered with toasted pecans and some wheat thins on the bar, and when I came back in, there was a small glob of cheese ball, no pecans, sitting in the middle of the plate, on the bar! I assume you both liked toasted pecans!

You gave us so many memories and so much joy, and now our lives have been blessed with Ava! She is so special and so loved.

I could go on and on, but I just want you to know that on this, your birthday, how you have blessed our lives and how much we love you.

HAPPY BIRTHDAY with LOVE,
Grandma Bo

Christmas Past

Christmas has come and gone
But the Spirit of love lingers on.

"Peace, good will", the angel said;
As the Babe lay in a manger bed.

God sent His Son, a Sign of Love
He came to earth from heaven above.

He is our Savior, Lord and King
Who came to cleanse us from everything
That separates and keeps us bound.
Though Christmas is past, may we hear the sound,
Of Angel choirs all year round.

Come, Holy Spirit; inspire our hearts with praise
As we remember God's gift in all our ways.
We rejoice in our hearts as we share
This blessed message everywhere.

Seasons of My Spirit

Autumn….vibrant….alive,
a hint of frost….
abundant gathering…the harvest.
Glorious tapestry…scarlet, gold, brown.
Leaves flutter to the ground and lie
accomplished, fulfilled…
as the autumn of my spirit.

Winter….its icy breath leaves me
chill and empty.
Groping for warmth.
Somewhere fire on the hearth; but ashes.
On the ground of stone, leaves…
brown, lifeless, crushed under foot.
And so….the winter of my spirit.

Spring….Life!
Stretching, longing, throbbing to escape.
Barren branches bursting,
buds; a promise.
Awakening, anticipation…

the rush of being alive
invades my spirit and settles into…

Summer…the season of growth.
Time….Sunshine….Rain.
Plains awash with waves of grain.
Ripening sheath, fruit, and flower
clutch completeness.
as summer breathes into fruition
the seasons of my spirit.

It matters not the season or time
without Your Spirit, Lord, my soul
is ever out of rhyme.
Summer, autumn, winter, spring.
Fruition, harvest, chill, groping…
awakening to Your Presence, Your grace
brings peace, joy…completeness.

Storms

The sudden storms of life
are like a tempest on the sea.
The fierce, swirling, frothy waves
come crashing down on me.
How swiftly tranquil situation
can turn into adversity.

I call for You, I cry in prayer.
Are You awake, God? Don't You care?
Though wind and wave may pound
I know You do care if I drown.
Ship-wreck is not the goal;
but faith in Him Who makes me whole.

For it is You, who gives direction
and rides with me in the strife.
When uncertain seas unsettle,
in faith I look to You, who rules
the wind and waves with but a word.
Peace, be still, comes from you, Oh, Lord!

Lines on Wynn Bullock's Photograph, "Forest"

I enter uninvited
Quietly, reverently
Ethereal cathedral
Mist embraced
Spires reaching upward
Sun's fingertips gently touch
With brightness and beauty
The lush, verdant view
Fern-fronds beckon escape
From humanity's madness

The cool, quiet stillness
The solitude
The enduring strength and majesty
Of this resplendent place
Fill me with awe and wonder
I wait…
I feel Divinity's Presence

Poetry is Like the Ocean

Poetry is like the waters of the ocean
that seem from a distance serene.
But the ocean is never still.
Waves lap against the shore
on days of calm
pound amid the storm.

Poetry flows from the depth
of the soul
and washes the beaches of the mind..
Word-pictures scurry like sand-crabs.
Images sometimes shallow, skimming the surface,
or so deep and vast, you can sail for days.

Walk along the shore view
the constantly moving, changing moods.
Glean treasures for your day
sea shells, starfish, stones and pebbles,
pieces of wreckage, huge logs brought by
the current from miles away.

Poetry, like the ocean is filled with life
tiny, insignificant, or huge as whales.
Look. See. There on the crest of a wave
or dive to the deep to catch a glimpse.
How old are the words? How old is the sea?

Trust

Fragile crystal gleaming
Rainbow mirrors shine
Heirloom treasure, mine.

Hearts touch, feel, care
Love grows
Years come, years go.

Love deepens
Trust, faith, unquestioning

Shattered
As crystal
No treasure
Pain, tears, aching heart.

Forgiveness, the rare adhesive
As you gather tiny pieces
Shyly, patiently, gently.

Can hearts heal?
Can trust be restored?

Pieces fit together
Almost

Fragile crystal gleaming
Never again
No rainbows

Years come, years go.

A Handful of Snake

Little did I know on that beautiful November day that I would have a nightmarish experience. The day started cool and crisp, a perfect day to mulch all the shrubbery. Distributing the pile of pine straw, I realized that the St. Augustine grass had sent runners through the shrubbery and those runners had reached the wall of the house. Reaching behind the shrubbery and pulling up the runners, I was advancing fairly well when I reached the sharp, prickly low holly that grows very near the house in front of the large living room window. A short handled rake was in the wheel barrow and by placing it behind the shrubbery and leaning on it, the sharp holly leaves would not stick my midsection. I was about half-way down and had developed a rhythm. Rake down, grab and lean, pull runners. Rake down, grab and lean, pull...oh, no! Instead of runners, I grabbed a handful of living, writhing, thrashing monster of a snake!

Falling backward, the yellowish underbelly of a huge snake was clearly visible as the rake literally walked across the window. There was nothing nearby to use to kill it, only that short handled rake and a few hand tools. If that snake got away, my yard work would most likely be over. Not wanting to take my eyes off the monster, I remembered the cordless phone lying on the ground and called my mother, who lived less than a mile away. "Hurry, Mother, I just grabbed a huge snake in front of the house and don't have anything to use to kill it!"

As Mother drove up the driveway, the unmistakable odor of musk filled the air. There was now no doubt that this was a cottonmouth, a highly poisonous snake, native to the south. Trying to point to where the snake was now entwined in some of the lower branches of holly, Mother strode up to about eighteen inches from where it was. As she parted the shrubbery, she said, "Are you sure it was a snake? I don't see anything!" "Get back, Mother, it is right there," I screamed! "Go to the greenhouse and get a hoe and shovel. Let me keep my eyes on that monster." Laughing, she shook her head and headed for the greenhouse. It was obvious that Mother did not believe me or at best thought I was exaggerating.

When Mother returned, I took the shovel and tried to cut into the snake, whacking and whacking. That big fellow was not going down easily. Trembling, and using the hoe, I was finally able to drag the snake out of the shrubbery. Mother's eyes were as big as saucers. She let out a few rarely used words of profanity and apologized. She said, "No wonder I didn't see it; I was looking for a snake, not a monster!" This handful of snake was forty nine and a half inches long; its head was almost six inches across and its midsection was as large as my husband's upper arm.

Most likely, I had placed the rake on the snake's head and with my weight on the rake handle, it had been unable to bite me. That would also explain the appearance of the rake walking across the window. To put it nicely, this experience actually enhanced my disdain of reptiles. Even today, when working with pine straw or digging in the flower beds, I anxiously look around and make lots of noise before proceeding. Many nights, there have been nightmares about grabbing and feeling the writhing and thrashing of that snake in my hand.

My Dairy Experience

"Got Milk?" We are all familiar with this advertising campaign encouraging the purchase of milk. We have seen scores of celebrities with their milk mustaches. The journey from the cow to the table is a labor intensive process for someone, but most people never give it a thought. In our society today, we take so many common, everyday conveniences for granted, and milk is certainly one of them. Of course, today's modern dairies are a far cry from the dairy of my growing-up years. Many think that nothing tastes better with a peanut butter and jelly sandwich or with chocolate chip cookies than a glass of ice cold milk. Having grown up on a dairy farm, I have a very different opinion of milk, based on my experience with cows.

Cows are the most stubborn animals ever put on this earth. A cow will not go anywhere she does not want to go or do anything she does not want to do. When there is a herd of about thirty to forty cows, each refusing to cooperate, it creates chaos. When I was a girl, one of my jobs was getting the cows from the pasture to the lot. The lot was a fairly large, tall enclosure, fenced with thick boards to contain the cows overnight. Cows must be milked morning and evening every day no matter the weather – hot, freezing and in between. Cows and calves are separated a week or so after birth. If they stayed together, the calves would get all the milk, so we would have a limited number of nursing cows. When I would get the cows to the lot, I would have to cut out the nursing cows and get them into one section of the barn, secure them in their stanchions, feed them and let the calves in to nurse. Most cows nursed from two to four calves; this was dependent on the amount of milk they gave and the age of the calves. When they finished, they had to be separated again and penned.

Then, I would go back to the lot and drive in the cows to be milked. Most would go immediately to their stanchions, but there would always be a few trouble makers. Once they were secured, I would then help pour feed into each trough and tend any injured or sick cows. Each cow had to be curried, brushed and during the summer, sprayed for flies. When that was done their bags had to be washed. This was not so bad during summer, but at three-thirty in the morning during the winter, it was awful. My hands would be so cold. I understand that today water and barns are heated; however, this was not so when I was a girl.

Reaching the main point of the entire process, the actual milking, I would grab a bucket and a stool and get into position. Often one of the ole hussies would try to kick me. There was a metal contraption that could be placed just above her hocks to keep her from kicking either me or the milk bucket, and she would try to kick out my brains the entire time it was being put in place. The next thing the cow would do was to whop me in the face with her tail. In summer her tail was usually full of cockle burrs, and in winter it was often frozen. Being too little to put her tail in the bend of my knee like Daddy did, I would get a hay string, loop it over the end of her tail and put the hay string in the bend of my knee. When the milk was squirted into the bucket, the foam would rise and the odor of the warm milk was almost nauseating. Finished, I would empty my bucket into the large milk can with the filtering funnel on top. Daddy would move the large cans into the milk room and replace them with empties as needed.

The next chore was to drive the cows out of the barn. In the evening, they stayed in the lot, but in the morning they were turned out to pasture. Then it was time to shovel the manure into a wheel barrow and empty the wheel barrow onto the manure pile. After this was done, we would have to hose down the floor, take heavy industrial brooms and disinfectant, scrub and rinse. We would be finished, at last, but only until the next time. After the morning milking, I would hurry into the house, clean up, get dressed, eat breakfast and run to catch the school bus. Sometimes on the bus I remember thinking that I still smelled like a dairy.

My dairy experience has definitely influenced my attitude about milk. Sometimes, even now, when I open a gallon of milk, I can still smell that dairy and it is not just the manure either. Cows have a distinctive odor, dependent on what they have been eating. Baby calves, feed, warm milk, all contribute to the overall odor of a dairy. The heat, the cold and all that hard work are indelibly stamped in my memory. When people talk about the good ole days, I shudder. I love getting milk from the grocery store for my family. Right now, I think I will have a cup of coffee.

Knowledge vs. Wisdom

We live in the so-called information age. We have more information today than we know how to process or use. For all of our information, have we increased in wisdom? We only need to look at recent history to gain an understanding that knowledge and wisdom are different. The Merriam-Webster Dictionary defines knowledge as "the accumulation of information" and wisdom as "the ability to discern or judge what is true, right, or lasting."

    The quest for knowledge is within reach of normal people. A teacher, a book, or a website can provide someone with a vast number of facts. The individual must either memorize these facts or understand how a certain concept works in order to achieve the solution to a problem. Once they do that they may be inclined to feel really smart, but they may not necessarily be wise. Knowledge and intelligence go together and will enable one to master a subject. One can be brilliant in academics, an expert in computers and technology, know how to build a house, or run a business…and know nothing about relationships, self-discipline, or what it takes to live a full life. There are numbers of highly educated, highly accomplished, highly talented, very well-informed people who have made foolish decisions and choices, and the result has been catastrophic for them and their families. Many times they find themselves stunned by the negative consequences of unwise choices and decisions.

In the deep wisdom of life, there are things to be learned that cannot be taught. We never know them by hearing them spoken or reading them, but we grow into them by experience. Experience alone does not guarantee wisdom; otherwise all the elderly would be wise. Life, then, is a counselor and wisdom is filtered through personal experience. Dietrich Bonhoeffer writes,

> "To understand reality is not the same as to know about outward events. It is to perceive the essential nature of things. The best-informed man is not necessarily the wisest. Indeed there is a danger that precisely in the multiplicity of his knowledge he will lose sight of what is essential. But on the other hand, knowledge of

an apparently trivial detail quite often makes it possible to see into the depth of things. And so the wise man will seek to acquire the best possible knowledge about events, but always without becoming dependent upon this knowledge. To recognize the significant in the factual is wisdom." Some people with great wisdom have had very little formal education, but they have a keen ability to discern and perceive…and their wise choices and decisions have led them to become powerful, influential, and successful.

Almost everyone acquires some wisdom during the course of his or her life. A wise person does not know everything, but a wise person is capable of using knowledge to maximum advantage. All of us face crises and calamities. Certainly, none of us succeed at everything all the time, but wisdom does help us to move through difficulty, hardship, and suffering and emerge stronger. Knowledge gives us facts; wisdom tells us what to do with these facts.

Persuasive Speech given in Public Speech Class at MCC
April 28, 2009

Introduction

I. If you were to win 2.4 million dollars in the lottery, would it make you happy?

    A. Most of you probably think it would.

    B. It would certainly enable you to pursue happiness very comfortably.

    C. In my class room survey, the majority of you responded that you are very happy most of the time.

    D. Completing the sentence, "The key to happiness is", was the most interesting response as there were fifteen different answers, and this would indicate that happiness is different for each one of you.

II. Today I want to persuade you to look seriously at your own happiness.

III. An article in an issue of "Psychology Today" entitled "The Pursuit of Happiness" by Carlin Flora, caught my attention and as I read it, I began to examine my own ideas of happiness and what my years have taught me.

   A. The article began, "Welcome to the happiness frenzy...." and went on to say that 4000 books on happiness were published last year, while only "50 books on the topic were released in 2000."
   B. It seems that as the "happiness movement has flourished", our nation has grown more anxious and sadder.

IV. I will convince you to consider your own happiness based on three things; what happiness is not, what happiness is and share some words of wisdom and some observations that will guide you to a lifetime of happiness.

(Let me begin with some of the things that happiness is not.)

Body

I. In her article, Ms Flora states, "Happiness is not about smiling all the time."

   A. It is not having a glib Pollyanna attitude that views everything that happens as good.

   B. It is not about doing away with bad moods or sadness.
      1. Life will present difficulties and challenges.
      2. You will feel a full range of emotions.
      3. There will be sadness, pain, disappointments and loss.

   C. Happiness is not getting everything you want.
      1. I mentioned winning the lottery and many think that it would solve all their problems and they would live "happily ever after."
      2. According to ABC's John Stossel, "Studies of

lottery winners found that within a year, most say they are no happier than they were before they won."

3. Craig Ziemba in his Easter column in "The Meridian Star" compares children scrambling to stuff their Easter baskets to adults who spend their lives in a "mad dash for bigger houses, fancier cars"....and burning themselves out "earning degrees, accomplishments, and recognition" thinking that if they "crammed their baskets full enough, they'd be happy"; but not even all these things guarantee happiness.

D. In response to negative feelings, many tend to grab quick fixes such as buying something you can't afford or eating something really fattening; while these instant indulgences might make you feel better for a few minutes, they leave you more miserable in the long run.

(It's important to realize what happiness is not: now let me tell you some of the things that happiness is.)

II. In answer to the question, "What is happiness?", Ms Flora writes, "The most useful definition—and it's one agreed upon by neuroscientists, psychiatrists, behavioral economists, positive psychologists, and Buddhist monks—is more like satisfied or content than "happy" in its strict bursting-with-glee sense."

A. She further explains that it has depth and deliberation and "encompasses living a meaningful life, utilizing your gifts and your time, living with thought and purpose."
B. She goes on to stress the importance of feeling part of a community, facing crisis with grace, and learning to stretch and grow.
C. Happiness is setting goals and anticipating achieving them.
D. Happiness is getting off the treadmill, where with each accomplishment, you keep plodding on for something you feel is still missing.
E. Happiness is simplifying your lives and making time for the truly important things.
F. Happiness is living according to your values.

(Now that you know what happiness is not and what it is let me finish with some words of wisdom that can send you on your journey to real happiness.)

III. Abraham Lincoln once said, "Most folks are about as happy as they make up their minds to be."

    A. Assuming that this is true, your happiness depends on you and your attitudes.

    B. Everyone is not fortunate enough to be born happy, but can learn to engage in mental dialogue to put down fearful and negative thoughts.

    C. There is no one-size-fits-all approach to happiness and pressure to cope with life in a way that doesn't fit not only doesn't work, but makes one feel like a failure in addition to already feeling bad.

    D. Happiness, as a goal, reminds me of my puppy chasing a butterfly.

        1. Just when the puppy gets close, the butterfly flutters away and is always just out of reach.

        2. When you pursue happiness, it seems to always be just out of reach, but by understanding more about yourselves and what brings real and

lasting happiness, you have a better chance of experiencing it.

(You now have enough information to be convinced that real and lasting happiness can be yours.)

Conclusion

I. In closing, I hope that this information will cause each of you to give serious thought to what it takes to achieve your own happiness.

II. When you live a meaningful life, use your time and gifts wisely, are willing to learn, stretch and grow, happiness will be a byproduct.

III. I would like to close with a quote from the King James Version of the Bible, Proverbs 3:13, "Happy is the man that findeth wisdom, and the man that getteth understanding."

My Favorite Place as a Child

My favorite place as a child was on the front porch of my grandparents' old house, sitting in the swing with my Grandma. The house was large, the paint dried and cracked, and the porch extended almost around the entire house. I spent many happy hours in that swing with Grandma. Her odor was of "sweet soap", as she called it and whatever she had cooked last. Sometimes, she smelled of fried ham, turnip greens, or vanilla - if she had baked tea cakes. She had been a school teacher before she married, and I was her first grandchild. She read to me and told stories about her childhood. Her favorite book was the Bible and she encouraged me to memorize numerous passages of scripture. From Grandma's swing, memories were created that will last a lifetime.

Grandma taught me many things, especially to observe and give thanks for the beauty of God's creations, and for the flow of the seasons, even the winter's cold barren landscape. The spring brought a time of rebirth, as the woods and pastures sported a coat in many shades of green, and the front yard was covered with a soft blanket of yellow daffodils. We watched the pastures for new babies; when the cows gave birth to new calves that romped and cavorted. The horses foaled, and we laughed at the long-legged foals as they wobbled about. The old hens would hatch tiny baby chicks, and it bothered me that these precious yellow balls of fluff would soon be cooped and fattened for frying!

Summer arrived with sweltering heat, but there always seemed to be a breeze on that porch. The air was filled with the fragrance of newly mowed hay; soon summer would slip away. Almost imperceptibly, a hint of chill in the air could be felt; fall had begun. Across the road, goldenrods filled an empty field and lined the edges of the pastures and fields with gold. Considered a weed by many, they were beautiful to me, and Grandma sang a little chorus about the goldenrods that ended with these words; "Or did the baby stars one night, come down and cover you?" Even in the cold of winter, Grandma would wrap me in a blanket, hold me close, as we sat in that wonderful swing. Even now, I seem to feel that swing slowly moving, chain squeaking, floor creaking, as Grandma would place her feet, heel, then toe; she caused the gentle rhythm of the motion of the swing. Probably, the most memorable part of this was the time and love lavished on me by Grandma.

The highlight of many days was the arrival of the postman. He brought publications that often contained a section called, "For the Wee Folk". In this section was printed "Picture and Word Stories" that I loved. From these, I began my journey of education and learned the magic of reading. There were also letters from far-away places, such as Grandma's sister, who lived in Los Angeles, California, and her brother, who was a railroad conductor and lived in Denver, Colorado. She had visited them several times and she would read portions of their letters and tell me about the Pacific Ocean and the Rocky Mountains. She had a friend, who was a missionary in China, and her letters were especially exciting for a little girl, living on a farm in rural Mississippi.

The sunsets of all the seasons were breathtaking, and we would sit enraptured by the colors that painted the sky: gold, yellows, oranges, pinks, and even shades of purple. Then, as the sky darkened, twilight descended and the sounds of crickets, frogs, and even an occasional whippoorwill would lull me into a sense of safety and comfort. The setting sun was soon swallowed by darkness. Nighttime had arrived. The stars appeared in the heavens and the man-in-the-moon seemed to smile.

Words not written by me, but words that inspire me

It is not you who shape God;

it is God that shapes you.

If then you are the work of God,

await the hand of the Artist

Who does all things in due season.

Offer the Potter your heart,

soft and tractable,

and keep the form in which

the Artist has fashioned you.

Let your clay be moist,

lest you grow hard and lose

the imprint of the Potter's fingers.

By Irenaeus, 2nd century theologian

The Search for Identity, Power, and Freedom Scratching a 55 Year Itch

The search for Identity, Power, and Freedom (IPF) was brought to this land of America even before colonies were established. These individuals came seeking religious freedom, economic gain, to avoid debtor's prison, to escape religious persecution, and to escape the tyrannical rule of kings and princes of Europe. Americans had great expectations for themselves and many Europeans spoke of their enthusiasm. The fact that their increase in business and population was not surprising and as they settled into the New World, they were sure all their success was the will of God. At first the higher purposes of their efforts were clear, but the founders agreed that the structure of government should reflect the structure of society. Maintaining this arrangement seemed desirable to Americans because "it conformed to the ancient British constitution, the most glorious frame of government yet devised by man". (MiddleKauff, 2005, p. 5-6) Yet, the assumptions about this fixed order for American colonials and England, seemed to diverge, as a fresh new society had begun to make an appearance in these colonies.

In the early eighteenth century, American colonists owed allegiance to the King of England and this connection did not restrict them. Then, the question arose of how men should be governed, if they were free men, should they not govern themselves.

There had been some conflict before, but now a long-standing resentment against external control came into play. England was three thousand miles away and the slowness of communication became an issue. Even before 1776, the Americans had almost become self governing through their provincial assemblies or legislature, and local governments that gave order to their lives.

Thomas Paine in his pamphlet, *Common Sense*, wrote, "The cause of America is in a great measure the cause of all mankind". He further states, "…is the Concern of every Man to whom Nature hath given the Power of feeling". He is not only addressing the identity, power, and freedom of the colonists, but of all mankind. Each individual must determine one's own identity.

Identities change over the course of a lifetime. For many years, I gave little thought to my identity. I was the older daughter in my family; then I became the wife, homemaker, mother, and grandmother. I just did what needed to be done. As a wife, mother, homemaker, I cooked, cleaned, washed, ironed, gardened, canned, and sewed.

I served as president of almost everything in which I was involved: the PTA, Symphony League, Junior Auxiliary, and two literary clubs. As the children grew up, I began to grow restless. My husband worked hard in his business and provided a good living, but our savings and investments remained minimal. I read some books on investing in real estate. My husband went to Atlanta one week on business and I bought a house. When he returned, he was shocked and none too happy. In the 70s and early 80s, women had a difficult time obtaining financing but I was able to find a lending institution that would work with me. I eventually obtained over ten rental units and did very well during the time I rented them, and also when I liquidated.

This peaked my interest in real estate and I obtained my broker's license and sold real estate for several years. I eventually became Executive Officer for the Meridian Board of REALTORS and was awarded the state scholarship to attend the National Association of REALTORS, Association Executive Institute where I was certified in Board Administration and Technology. I later retired from that position.

Now, I am a student! I am scratching a 55 year itch. Let me explain; when I answered a bonus question on a test, my tenth grade English teacher had told me that I was definitely college material, since I was the only student in all of her years of teaching that had answered that question correctly. I was elated and could not wait to get home and tell my mother. As I hurried into the house, she was in the kitchen and I told her immediately what Mrs. Chance had told me. I will never forget my mother's words, "I ought to go and give that woman a piece of my mind! The very idea, you better get those notions out of your head, cause there's no way in hell, you will go to college"! I was crushed. Those words haunted me for 55 years and then in 2007, at the age of 71, I enrolled in Meridian Community College. I had hoped to go to college earlier, but had no financial or moral support. My husband could see no reason for me to attend college, since I was a homemaker, and mother, and I did not need college for that! Having no income of my own, college seemed out of the question. Then my father and mother died within eight months of each other and I inherited their home, which I rented out; this gave me the financial means to pursue my dream of an education. The responses of friends and relatives have been interesting: from "Wow, I think that is wonderful. I am so proud of you!" to "Have you lost your mind?"

I have learned so much in my years in college and not all has been from books. The association with other students has greatly enhanced my quality of life. To the young students, I would counsel, "Seize the opportunities as they are presented!" I have also found that not all youth are represented by what the media shows. Many long-time norms have been challenged by exposure to others. I have a new and different relationship with my spouse of 61 years. He still does not understand why, but he's proud of me!

To define my identity, I would have to say the most important to me is that I am a Christian. I never remember not knowing that God loved me and Christ died for me.

As I look back over my life, I realize I am strong; I have persevered through severe physical abuse as a child, the death of my only brother and younger son, both at young ages. I must be a leader, having served as president of so many organizations and having taught Sunday school for many years. There is power in determining ones identity, and with power, one has more freedom to do and be what ever one is willing to dream and work toward. I can honestly say that I do not know how to quit! As for scratching a 55 year itch, it feels good!

Speech I made when installed as President of the Meridian Symphony League, May, 1971:

As I accept this gavel from Julia, I find my mind filled with a kaleidoscope of thoughts. Memories of things past, a sense of pride and accomplishment in things present and high hopes for the future.

A while back I read these pointers on public speaking: "Be brief, be sincere, be seated." This is the outline I plan to follow.

A week or so ago, I was sitting on my bed, surrounded by papers, formulating plans for the coming year, several telephone calls were made, then I leaned back and closed my eyes a moment, my daughter, who had been sitting in a chair quietly observing, said, "Mother, why are you doing all this?" I said, "You know I'll be president of the League

Board this coming year." She replied, "That's what I mean, why do you do all this junk?" I began to think, why do I do all this, why do you do? Surely, the basic reason must be a love of music. Music washes the dust from the soul of everyday life. The one common and universal language is music. By music, man may express every emotion and determine his ideals. Plato has said, "Music is a moral law. It gives a soul to the universe, wings to the mind, flight to the imagination, a charm to sadness, gayety and life to everything. It is the essence of order, and leads to all that is good, just, and beautiful."

Our orchestra does give us beautiful music and we appreciate them and our conductor, Mr. Vernon Raines.

As I thought, I remembered the League Board and the Larger League, the cooperation, the willingness, the work, for truly these are the "workingest" women you ever saw! Coming together is a beginning, keeping together is progress, working together is success. So in this sense the League is truly a success. But we cannot rest on our laurels. Each year we build on the foundations that have already been laid. Neither could I forget the Society

Board, a group of busy people. They act as advisors, administrators, providers and supporters. I had no idea of the work involved until I had the opportunity to observe first hand.

If I could ask only one thing of you for the year 1971-72, it would have to be ENTHUSIASM. You cannot kindle a fire in any other heart until it is burning within your own. Apathy can only be overcome by enthusiasm, and enthusiasm can only be aroused by two things; first, an ideal that takes the imagination by storm, and second, a definite intelligible plan for carrying that ideal into practice. I ask of you enthusiasm and enthusiasm I shall receive, for I have that kind of faith in you. Life would not be worth living without faith: faith in God; faith in our self; faith in our fellowmen. Without faith in God, there is no hope for the soul; without faith in self, life is a miserable failure; without faith in each other we should miss the sweet joys of friendship.

So as we embark upon the voyage of a new year, may you remember these words: cooperation, willingness, work, faith and above all enthusiasm.

Mississippi Is

Vine-ripened tomatoes, fresh, tender corn
Mist above the water in the early morn

Barefoot boy running with his dog
Violets blooming by a fallen log

Thunder sounds rumble from afar
Lightning bugs blinking in a jar

Cows, calves and horses in the pasture
Glorious sunsets to behold in rapture

The place I love and time to rest
My home in Mississippi is surely best

A Cardinal Blessing

A flash of crimson on a dreary day
Feathered wings spread in flight
Brilliantly reflected in the light
He surveys the banquet feast spread
Gently alights, for his daily bread
Wearing his crown, this majestic bird
Brings joy to my heart without a word.

Worn-out Work Boots

Memories evoked, emotions stirred.

"What do you mean?" Some might ask;

Worn-out work boots on a pile of trash?

Ask any cattleman's wife

Whose cowboy is still the love of her life.

Those boots symbolize commitment, devotion

As they have provided protection

Through heat, drought, and flood

Snow, ice, and mud.

When the tornado came and

Destroyed trees, barn, and fences.

Everyone slowly came to their senses

Boots were pulled on and work begun

Day after day 'til all was done.

That is how these boots became worn

No orders or rules to be heeded

Simply doing the work that was needed.

CPSIA information can be obtained
at www.ICGtesting.com
Printed in the USA
LVHW092119141021
700495LV00001B/18